Psychopaths and Institutions

Lonnie Hicks

ISBN: SBN-13: 978-1499796575
ISBN-10: 1499796579

Forward

There is a growing body of literature which makes the argument that certain institutions attract, breed and promote and are headed by psychopathic personality types.

Could this be true?

Let's look at the literature and the studies and decide for ourselves.

Is Civilization the product of Psychopathic Thinking?

http://rense.com/general83/twi.htm

Who is, and what is, a psychopath?

"Evidence collected by psychologists paints a very clear picture. Psychopaths are masters at manipulating people. They have the uncanny ability to conceal their predatory and emotionless tendencies behind a magnetic personality and an arsenal of lies. And it is nearly universal that they desire power over others, if simply for the sake of using that power. Many of these people, which represent between 2 and 12 million Americans, are able to rise to the top of politics, banking, business, and military with their psychopathy hiddMany other psychopaths are born into the position of power; their fathers were psychopaths and their grandfathers were psychopaths."

From:

http://www.thepeopleshistory.net/2013/08/psychopathy-power-and-politics.html?m=1

http://www.cassiopaea.com/cassiopaea/psychopath3.htm

http://www.cassiopaea.org/cass/political_ponerolo
gy_lobaczewski.htm

http://www.decision-making-
confidence.com/what-is-a-psychopath.html

http://www.systemsthinker.com/interests/mind/psy
chopathy.shtml

http://bjp.rcpsych.org/content/182/1/5.full

http://www.thestar.com/opinion/editorialopinion/2
011/11/23/weeding_out_corporate_psychopaths.ht
ml

http://en.wikipedia.org/wiki/Criticisms_of_corpora
tions

http://idealoblog.blogspot.com/2011/05/interlude-
all-of-them-witches.html

http://www.thepeopleshistory.net/2013/08/psychop
athy-power-and-politics.html

Revolution? Video
http://gawker.com/russell-brand-may-have-started-
a-revolution-last-night-1451318185

The Financial Crisis of 2008 and Psychopathic
Thinking

http://www.ritholtz.com/blog/2012/01/psychopaths-caused-the-financial-crisis/

http://idealoblog.blogspot.com/2012/01/you-dont-have-to-be-psychopath-to-work.html

http://www.commondreams.org/headlines04/0120-03.htm

http://archneurpsyc.jamanetwork.com/article.aspx?articleid=652271#Abstract

The Military and the Psychopathic Thesis
http://rense.com/general83/twi.htm

Psychopaths in the Context of the Family
https://www.lovefraud.com/2012/08/25/sociopaths-victimize-using-human-institutions-like-the-courts/

Studies:

http://www.sciencedaily.com/releases/2013/07/130724200412.htm

http://www.sciencedaily.com/releases/2013/09/130924174331.htm

http://www.sciencedaily.com/releases/2013/04/130424161108.htm

10-28-13
Psychopaths and the Family

https://www.lovefraud.com/2012/08/25/sociopaths
-victimize-using-human-institutions-like-the-
courts/

10-29/13

The Psychopathic Organization: The Enron
Example

Enron as a case study of a psychopathic
corporation and the psychopathic culture

http://books.google.com/books?id=g62S9V7xdTE
C&pg=PT156&lpg=PT156&dq=psychopaths+and
+institutions&source=bl&ots=rVbsEEkVKQ&sig
=mC35FJlcA8ymFVn8C1fngssMwMM&hl=en&s
a=X&ei=PE5xUtKoCITZigKlloDABg&ved=0CD
AQ6AEwBjgK#v=onepage&q=psychopaths%20a
nd%20institutions&f=false

The Corporation As Psychopathic Actor

http://siivola.org/monte/papers_grouped/uncopyrig
hted/Misc/corporate_psychopathy.htm

10/29/13

Psychopaths and Society-Historical Examples

http://www.ageofaquarius.cc/psychopaths.php

10/30/13

Details of the Psychopathic Personality

http://www.softcom.net/users/greebo/psychopath.htm

10/30/13

Are You or Are You Dating A Psychopath? Video: How to Tell.

http://zazenlife.com/2013/07/11/are-you-a-psychopath/

10/31/13

Does the banking and insurance industries actively recruit psychopaths?
Banking and Insurance Clusters-Do They Actively Recruit Psychopaths?

http://nelsnewday.wordpress.com/2013/06/22/psyc

hopaths-cluster-at-the-top/

"Brian Basham said a banking colleague once confided to him, "At one major investment bank for which I worked, we used psychometric testing to recruit social psychopaths because their characteristics exactly suited them to senior corporate finance roles." Insurance companies also suffer from the psychopaths in their leadership."

More on Corporate Psychopaths:

http://www.americanthinker.com/2011/12/the_corporate_psychopaths_among_us.html

10/31/13

The View of Psychopaths in Kubrick Films

www.americanthinker.com/2011/12/the_corporate_psychopaths_among_us.html
"While the psychopath has likes and dislikes and fondness for the pleasures that human company can bring, analysis shows that he is completely egocentric, valuing others only for their enhancement of his own pleasure or status. While he gives no real love, he is quite capable of inspiring love of sometimes fanatical degree in others. He is generally superficially charming and often makes a striking impression as possessed of

the noblest of human qualities. He makes friends easily, and is very manipulative, using his ability with words to talk his way out of trouble. Many psychopaths love to be admired and bask in the adulation of others. With the lack of love, there is also a lack of empathy. The psychopath is unable to feel sorry for others in unfortunate situations or put himself in another's place, whether or not they have been harmed by him."

From:
http://www.visual-memory.co.uk/amk/doc/0004.html

More on Kubrick Films

http://kubrickfilms.tripod.com/id15.html
Is Psychopathy inherited? Some say so.

10/31/13

Is Psychopathy Inherited?

"Are the psychopath, sociopath, and someone with the Antisocial Personality Disorder one and the same? The DSM says "yes". Scholars such as Robert Hare and Theodore Millon beg to differ. The psychopath has antisocial traits for sure but they are coupled with and enhanced by callousness, ruthlessness, extreme lack of empathy, deficient impulse control, deceitfulness, and sadism.

Like other personality disorders, psychopathy becomes evident in early adolescence and is considered to be chronic. But unlike most other personality disorders, it is frequently ameliorated with age and tends to disappear altogether in by the fourth or fifth decade of life. This is because criminal behavior and substance abuse are both determinants of the disorders and behaviors more typical of young adults.

Psychopathy may be hereditary. The psychopath's immediate family usually suffers from a variety of personality disorders."

From:

http://samvak.tripod.com/personalitydisorders16.html

11/1/13

The Female Psychopath. This is astounding.

http://www.whale.to/c/know_thy_self.html

"Typical Female Psychopathic Traits

- Unexpected sexual arousal
- Large clitoris
- Pronounced Adams Apple (by female standards)
- Waking up in pools of sweat even in cool weather
- Somewhat unfeminine posture when viewed from behind (but this is not a hard and fast rule)
- Violent or sadistic sexual requests (wanting their nipples bitten hard, etc.)
- Falling asleep and waking up instantly. Sleep and waking is instantaneous with all psychopaths

- Unexpected swing from idealization of male partners to almost instant cold rejection leaving one feeling shattered, confused and with symptoms similar to Post Traumatic Stress disorder which can last from months to years
- Extreme and Obvious Flattery. Emulating and Sycophantic Behavior *Lovebombing*, designed to release large amounts of dopamine and norepinephrine, while reducing low activity in serotonin within the victim's brain so that the victim becomes emotionally dependent on the

psychopath and thus becomes highly vulnerable to the psychopath's suggestions. The areas of the brain that produce dopamine become hyperactive, and are directly related to addictions. Since their teens, psychopaths have learned to manipulate their victims through this technique. The term lovebombing was brought into common usage by the psychologist Professor Margaret Singer in her book *Cults in Our Mids*t.

If you are a nice guy you are more of a target— they will often remark how kind and nice you are. This makes you easy prey. You will also find that the early sweet loving kindness performance of the female psychopath will be interrupted now and again with a nasty and mean performance. Then a cycle develops where the frequencies of the nasty state increases—while the kindness state become less and less. Eventually, from the height of loving, idealization and adoration the female psychopath obsessively showered you with in the early days—you will find yourself trapped in a negative, unloving and exploitative lifestyle not of your making."

Also:
"SMEAR CAMPAIGNS
She will spread negative and false rumors about you to her friends while garnishing sympathy from

her on-tap, plethora of female pity enablers who believe every negative statement about you which she tells them. The female psychopath also generally befriends less attractive, overweight, 'frumpy' and unstylish women in order for the female psychopath to look more attractive when in their company."

From:

http://www.whale.to/c/female_psychopaths.html

11/2/13
Psychopaths: What to Do?

http://www.youtube.com/watch?feature=player_detailpage&v=Hon3AzMO6vs

http://www.youtube.com/watch?feature=player_detailpage&v=SLz_U0RFRuo

http://www.youtube.com/watch?feature=player_detailpage&v=Pqe4SaVo7UI

The Five Red Flags of Psychopaths? The video

http://www.youtube.com/watch?feature=player_detailpage&v=p1uvXoX83dA

http://www.youtube.com/watch?v=SLz_U0R
FRuo

http://www.youtube.com/watch?feature=play
er_detailpage&v=O3cNFMXNyzQ

http://www.youtube.com/watch?v=lZP6YKn
xMHk

11/2/13

The Male Psychopathic
http://www.youtube.com/watch?feature=play
er_detailpage&v=jYP9JShyXAc

11/3/13

11/3/13 Were the Nazi Leaders Psychopathic
or "Normal?" A Report From Douglas Kelly,
psychiatrist, who examined Nazi leaders.

Kelly examined Nazi leaders after World
War 11 and was shocked to find them like us.

"The conclusions Dr. Kelly made are
frightening and still relevant to this day. In
his writings, Dr. Kelley stated that there was
nothing "special" about these top Nazis and
their personalities. What happened during
Germany's Third Reich could happen in
any country."

From:

http://www.seattlepi.com/lifestyle/blogcritics/
article/Book-Review-The-Nazi-and-the-
Psychiatrist-4907865.php

Kelly later also concluded that about half of
the American population was psychopathic in
the same way the Nazis were. Now that is
scary but consistent with the material we
have research above in this blog.

"[Kelley] believed that Goering and his
cohorts were commonplace people and that
their personalities 'could be duplicated in any
country of the world today,' "writes El-Hai.
"In the years before and during World War II,
the opportunity to obtain power led them to
embrace a chilling political philosophy. In
other words, the Holocaust and the wars other
heinous crimes were the products of healthy
minds."

From:

http://www.minnpost.com/second-
opinion/2011/01/nazi-war-criminal-us-
psychiatrist-and-commonplace-nature-evil

At some point we want to look at what can be done.

See video also:

https://www.goodreads.com/videos/50749-the-nazi-and-the-psychiatrist-book-trailer

11/3/13

Psychopathic Characters in Shakespeare?

Shakespeare and Psychopaths

http://voices.yahoo.com/manipulation-psychopath-shakespeare-6518736.html

http://timesupblog.blogspot.com/2010/09/iago-shakespeares-psychopath.html

"Psychopaths have been studied for centuries. In the mid-1800s, Philippe Pinel created the first written record of psychopaths. There is evidence of psychopaths in historical, religious, and literary texts. Surprisingly, the number of psychopaths is surprisingly high. In the United States, there is one psychopath in every 100 American. In Britain, there are two in every 100 British. Some psychologists claim that some social elites might also be psychopaths, including attorneys, politicians, doctors, and businessmen. Female psychopaths are rarer than male psychopaths. They are less violence than male psychopath and have a lower rate of recidivism."

From:

http://gracechenenglish2.blogspot.com/2012/12/macbeth-is-psychopath.html

11/4/13

How to cope with Narcissists and Psychopaths- Strategies- Videos

Coping Strategies for Psychopaths and Narcissists

http://www.youtube.com/watch?feature=player_detailpage&v=njxtBM0RQnM

http://www.youtube.com/watch?feature=player_detailpage&v=9u4KA4zEGiI

http://www.youtube.com/watch?feature=player_detailpage&v=jYP9JShyXAc

11/5/13

The Top Ten Professions Where Psychopaths are concentrated.

"The occupation with the highest proportion of psychopaths is CEO. Is it possible that though most engineers are middling in normality, the ones who rise to CEO are dangerously bonkers?

I fear it may be the case. Somehow, the need to grab power all for yourself might be revelatory.

It's fascinating, though, which other professions are on the list. Just behind CEOs come lawyers. The jokes do write themselves sometimes. Third on the list is media. Please, lower thy cudgel. This specifically refers to TV and radio media. We're looking at you, Sean Hannity and Jon Stewart.

Lower down we find salesperson (naturally), surgeon (they're mostly nuts), and then, well, journalist. That last one is probably a typo. Police officer, clergyperson, chef (good Lord, yes), and civil servant round out the Top 10."

From:

http://news.cnet.com/8301-17852_3-57610538-71/great-news-engineers-arent-psychopaths-but-ceos-are/

11/6/13

More on Female Psychopaths--Less is Known About Them Than Their Male Counterparts
"For example, these researchers found overlap between some of the symptoms such as histrionic personality disorder or borderline personality disorder. A woman whose extreme fear of abandonment leads her to periodic outbursts of rage over real or imagined transgressions, flips between seeing her significant other as either completely perfect or totally evil, or who has to constantly be the center of attention certainly isn't who we think of when we think of the classic psychopath. But she may be just as incapable of true empathy, and just as manipulative and deceitful, as the callous, unemotional male."

 From:

http://www.psychologytoday.com/blog/the-human-equation/201205/female-psychopaths

10/6/13
The Non-Criminal Psychopath   Ambulatory Psychopaths

The study of "ambulatory" psychopaths - what we call "The Garden Variety Psychopath" - has, however, hardly begun. Very little is known about *subcriminal psychopathy*. However, some researchers have begun to seriously consider the idea that it is important to study psychopathy not as an artificial clinical category but as a *general personality trait in the community at large*. In other words, psychopathy is being recognized as a more or less a *different type of human*.

One very interesting aspect of the psychopath is his "hidden life" that is sometimes not too well hidden. It seems that the psychopath has a regular need to take a "vacation into filth and degradation" the same way normal people may take a vacation to a resort where they enjoy beautiful surroundings and culture. To get a full feeling for this strange "need" of the psychopath - a need that seems to be evidence that "acting human" is very stressful to the psychopath - read more of **The Mask of Sanity, chapters 25 and 26.**

Also, read <u>Cleckley's speculations</u> on what was "really wrong" with these people. He comes very close to suggesting that they are human in every respect - but that they lack a soul."

From:

http://www.cassiopaea.com/cassiopaea/psychopath.htm

11/8/13

The Psychopath Personality Test: 20 questions to tell if you or someone you know is a psychopath.

http://www.arkancide.com/psychopathy.htm

11/13/13

The Ten Most Psychopathic Professions and the Ten Least Psychopathic Professions and Why.

http://www.policymic.com/articles/72653/these-are-the-10-most-psychopathic-jobs-in-america

"SCHIZOIDAL PSYCHOPATHY

"[Schizoids] are hypersensitive and distrustful, while, at the same time, pay little attention to the feelings of others. They tend to assume extreme positions, and are eager to retaliate for minor offenses. Sometimes they are eccentric and odd. Their poor sense of psychological situation and reality leads them to superimpose erroneous, pejorative interpretations upon other people's intentions. They easily become involved in activities which are ostensibly moral, but which actually inflict damage upon themselves and others. Their impoverished psychological worldview makes them typically

pessimistic regarding human nature."
(Lobaczewski, 123-4)"

A Social Analysis of Psychopaths

http://www.thepeopleshistory.net/2013/08/psychop
athy-power-and-politics.html

11/16/13

Dating Red Flags

http://nicoleodell.com/2013/11/dating-red-flags/

11/24/13
The Brain of the Psychopath:
http://www.sciencedaily.com/releases/2010/03/100
314150924.htm

11/25/13

Psychopaths and Sociopaths in dating. Love
Fraud-six videos

http://www.youtube.com/watch?feature=player_e
mbedded&v=kL24yoR2H2M

http://www.youtube.com/watch?feature=player_e
mbedded&v=kL24yoR2H2M

11/26/13

The Psychopath Next Door

http://www.youtube.com/watch?feature=player_detailpage&v=aFVrvoYTGu0

http://www.youtube.com/watch?feature=player_detailpage&v=O3cNFMXNyzQ

11/26/13
Defenses against Psychopaths Etc.

Part One
http://www.youtube.com/watch?feature=player_detailpage&v=XAwR6YVf4IE

Part Two
http://www.youtube.com/watch?feature=player_detailpage&v=8d2KloYNXl0

Part Three
http://www.youtube.com/watch?feature=player_detailpage&v=Ri2Wa7SW6k4

More spotting Psychopaths
http://www.youtube.com/watch?feature=player_detailpage&v=nMG1qjpzNPg

11/29/13

Seven signs to tell if your boss is a psychopath

http://www.huffingtonpost.com/kevin-dutton/boss-psychopath_b_2083799.html#slide=1725376

Signs of Psychopathy

http://crime.about.com/od/serial/a/psychopaths.htm

12/2/13

Questionnaire

http://crime.about.com/library/blpsychoquiz.htm

More on Female Psychopaths

http://datingasociopath.com/sociopath-character-traits/female-sociopath/

12/3/13 The Psychopathic Website

More on dating or being married to a psychopath

http://datingasociopath.com/2013/11/22/sociopathic-abuse/

Meantime see companion pieces below:

Unconscious America
http://www.authorsden.com/visit/viewshortstory.as
p?id=60169&authorid=121255

Blood Simple:
http://www.authorsden.com/visit/viewshortstory.as
p?id=52140&authorid=121255

1/6/14

Rome as a prime example of the psychopathic state
and of the Blood Simple society.

Hear Dan Carlin's excellent podcast on the Decline
of the Roman Empire. The best I audio I have
heard on this and over 10 hours long but worth it.

Riveting throughout and told in an incredibly
accessible style. You come away understanding
the Roman Empire and the psychopathic state.

http://www.dancarlin.com//disp.php/hharchive/Sho
w-34---Death-Throes-of-the-Republic-
I/%20podcast-Rome-Republican

http://www.dancarlin.com//disp.php/hharchive/Show-35---Death-Throes-of-the-Republic-II/%20podcast,Rome-Marius-Sulla

http://www.dancarlin.com//disp.php/hharchive/Show-36---Death-Throes-of-the-Republic-III/%20Rome-Marius-Sulla

http://www.dancarlin.com//disp.php/hharchive/Show-37---Death-Throes-of-the-Republic-IV/%20Rome-Marius-Sulla

http://www.dancarlin.com//disp.php/hharchive/Show-38---Death-Throes-of-the-Republic-V/%20Rome-Marius-Sulla

See also other audio by Dan Carlin

http://www.dancarlin.com/disp.php/hharchive

1/7/14

Carlin on the Mongol Empire. Scary Stuff. This guy is brilliant.

http://www.dancarlin.com//disp.php/hharchive/Show-43---Wrath-of-the-Khans-I/Mongols-Genghis-Chingis

http://www.dancarlin.com//disp.php/hharchive/Show-44---Wrath-of-the-Khans-II/Mongols-Genghis-Chingis

http://www.dancarlin.com//disp.php/hharchive/Show-45---Wrath-of-the-Khans-III/Mongols-Genghis-Chingis

http://www.dancarlin.com//disp.php/hharchive/Show-46---Wrath-of-the-Khans-IV/Mongols-Genghis-Chingis

1/8/14

Now we are in a position to begin to answer the questions above.

The ability of human beings to be completely inured to the suffering of others after prolonged immersion in violence seems to have been with the human race from the beginning.

Psychopathic leaders and their crimes have been with us a long, long time.

The users of violence do not, after a fashion, see others as human and treat them as animals-no worse than animals. We generally don't lop of the heads of animals for sport and as a terror tactic.

Sad to say that now several preliminary observations are possible.

This behavior in our history fits precisely the description of the psychopathic dynamic and more, gives us an answer as to how such leaders get followers to treat others inhumanely, make them also capable of psychopathic behavior as well.

Psychopathic leaders and the institutions and groups they head or influence, create psychopathic followers by treating them brutally, promising them money, wealth, women, power, prestige, honors and the like.

The brutality of this existence with its carrots and sticks allow the followers to take out the terrors of this existence on others which they willingly do.

Those that don't do it are killed, incarcerated, tortured, and most often driven out or wiped out.

The remaining followers adapt by becoming psychopaths themselves, or here in modern times, participate vicariously.

Some blind themselves and retreat inward, indulging in private pleasures, distractions or put blinders on, preferring not to see their actual situation in life and in the society.

Preferring not to see how their governments or their leaders are treating other peoples.

After a while all of this becomes embedded in culture of the society, in its laws, customs and philosophy.

We note that such a dynamic is also passed down within families; down the generations.

But note, a ray of hope is that the cultural component can, and often is, broken by changes in cultural norms.

That is, such behavior can be reduced, if not eliminated, by education, wealth-sharing, and exposure to other ways of being and other ideas and cultures.

It happened with the Mongols and the Romans.

Note, too, that terror as a way of life carries within it the seeds of its own eventual destruction.

Mongol will, and did turn on Mongol; Roman, will and did turn on Roman.

Terror toward others eventually leads to terror against each other and civil war.

 Note, too, that victims exposed to this behavior:

1. Can come to identify with the power and ruthlessness of their oppressors and can aspire to become one of the group.

2. Can become paralyzed in the face of the terror tactics of the pyschopathic group utilizes to control them.

3. Can fantasize about having secret super powers and fight back, in that fantasy world. Think comic books and many of the latest major movies featuring comic book heroes.

4. Can revolt but often do not have the same ruthlessness of the psychopathic group and often lose the battle, or, even if winning, have to then look to battle other psychopathic groups coming down the line.

5. Can with thousands of years of exposure to this kind of psychopathic environment, come to have it all lodged in the unconscious mind to haunt them in their fears, in patterns of anxiety, and wide-spread depression and feelings of hopelessness coupled with suppressed anger.

It is clear, at least to me, that the American society fits the description of these aspects and they sit there in plain sight.

But what to do? What are the counters to the psychopathic society?

1/10/14

Now before we go back to effects and counters, we want to take a look at the question of how psychopathic behavior and religion have managed to co-exist during all, if not most of this period, and in human history?

In the period prior to the advent of Christianity the pharaoh or king was considered divine, or in direct contact with gods, which may reside in the heavens or in nature itself.

The king or oracle interpreted the will of the gods or was a god himself and after death joined these other gods in the sky or below the earth or in some other location.

But with the advent of Christianity in the Roman empire the Christian message was clear: "thou shall not kill."

How was this to be reconciled-a brutal psychopathic state and a passivist religion?

Step one was, as interpreted by some, was to render unto Caesar those things which were Caesar's and render unto the Church or Christ those things belonging to Christ.

This compromise basically states earthly things belong to the powers of this world, while believers had to wait until the next life, or judgment day to right wrongs done them.

You can see how this benefited the psychopathic state. First religion told them to obey the local warlord or king because it was god's will working in everyday life.

Moreover, evil befalling the masses were likely God or the Gods punishing them for their sins.

This is a view still prevalent today in most western societies.

Religion has this understanding with the powers that be to this very day.

While revolts, religious in nature, have occurred against the state, such believers have been ruthlessly crushed and the church has often cooperated in labeling such rebels as "heretics" and killed or banished them in their millions.

The Church as always cooperated with the psychopathic state-at least most of the time.

Often religious wars as well have occurred, one lasting over 100 years. The Crusades come to mind as well as the current situation where some evangelistic churches see Islam as heretics and some Islamic believers see Christians as "infidels."

All of this, it can be argued, encapsulates much of Western history and Eastern History as well.

For details on some of this see:

http://english.ahram.org.eg/NewsContent/18/0/615 13/Books/Mixing-religion-and-politics-is-the-root-of-despot.aspx

http://www.onislam.net/english/shariah/contempor ary-issues/interviews-reviews-and-events/440660-the-dangers-of-religious-despotism.html

http://www.bu.edu/paideia/existenz/volumes/Vol.5 -1Dale.pdf

http://synapostasy.blogspot.com/2007/08/enlighten ed-despotism-and-liberal.html

We continue next time going into more trends and details.

1/11/14

The Religion-Psychopathic State accommodation
has been in place for centuries, if not most of the
history of mankind, and creates in the population a
particular form of brain development where:

The population disassociates moral strictures as
enunciated by Religion from the dictates of the all-
powerful Psychopathic State. The mind becomes
compartmentalized.

At work ruthlessness rules: but notes there is no
democracy at work or in the modern corporation:
but at home we preach democracy, in schools as
well, and we theoretically are loving, kind and
empathic as well in the latter two venues.

This is a schizoid existence.

This is yet another effect of the Psychopathic
State-it creates in the population an ability to be
incredibly cruel in one aspect, all the while
maintaining a pious self-concept in another
context.

Now this brings us back to Freud to examine
another effect.

Freud, as we see above makes the argument in
"Civilization and Its Discontents" that the ID, the

Super-Ego and the Ego provide the dynamic of the unconscious mind.

For definitions of the above three see:

http://en.wikipedia.org/wiki/Id,_ego_and_super-ego

Note that this notion of Freud's describes the human unconscious in exactly the way I have posited above-compartmentalized, schoizd and contradictory.

Now Freud's view is that this is simply built into the human psyche and all human beings have it, that it is part of the instinct structure of the human species.

My argument is that clearly this is not the case.

These divisions in the human psyche come from actual pressures in human society and that content of the human psyche comes from human experience in society.

Super-Ego is what is left of the moral aspect; the ID is the presence of psychopathic tendencies in a given society. Ego represents the dilemmas of this as individuals try to navigate life over the centuries.

Thus, the content of the human unconscious is the direct result of thousands of years of interactions in real societies with these issues.

Thus, seen this way vampires, the half dead, horror movies, murder, blood and other horrific items we see in American movies and on American TV (see the companion blog on this site "Unconscious America") are external manifestations of the real life circumstances of a given population, not the product of an undefined instinct, inborn within the human psyche as Freud claims.

Thus, real life experiences dictate the content of the unconscious, not instinct, and this is the good news--as cultural content changes in interaction with the social environment, this also initiates changes in the content of the unconscious.

Our look at the history of the most vicious empires in history show that even they are subject to change, from the Romans, to the Mongols, to Western and Eastern Societies down through history--they do change, admittedly, most often from internal divisions, or fall down from their own weight.

But must we wait hundreds of years for change? No.
There are other change factors in modern times

and we look at those next.
Next time.

1/15/14

But before we do this let's take a look at the last two topics we have explored-those of Religion and the Freudian analysis.

With Freud arguing that the unconscious content is driven by either individual neurosis or psychosis, accounting for all of this becomes individual or lodged somewhere in the mysterious unconscious.

The state, and societal conditions are not emphasized and we are left with individual solutions, not ones which involve societal change or challenges the status quo in any way.

The mental health of the individual is identified as the fault and preserve of the individual.

Individuality is promoted here but it is a false individuality masking an underlying suppression of what Freud regarded as dangerous instincts.

We have a similar outcome with the Religion compromise in that passivity in the face of the pyschopathic state is to be ignored, and in many cases cooperated with.

The net result is that the individual is isolated and powerless before the powerful state and unable to recognize or pursue community interests.

Couple these factors with a divide and rule tactic of the ruling king, pharaoh, or government and we have the broad outlines of much of Western and Eastern history.
Recognize that divide and rule works in this kind of society because many if not most of the citizens have been brutalized mentally, physically or psychologically such that each is suspicious of the other, work for the state or businesses involved and dependent upon these institutions for jobs and their life and livelihoods.

Most often this kind of population becomes attracted to sadism, masochism, or become its voyeurs.

But, again, what can, and what has been done, to turn around these states of affairs in the past?

What has worked?

Ok, next, we will take a look at the factors. Promise.

1/13/14

So what are the possibilities today which make the above pattern reversible?

1. Communication: Never before in the history of the world has it been easier to communicate and therefore to organize. Success becomes easier with this factor. The internet is a true revolution along with TV and other media. That makes it dangerous to the powers that be because millions can see what is occurring thousands of miles away and down the street as well.

2. Awareness: The Psychopathic State has become more and more exposed because this knowledge has become more available to many more folks. We can see it on our televisions each night.

The reaction to this, by social psychopaths, has been to shut down dissent.

This will in time back-fire because the violent mind-set created by the state, comes to operate against the state as well.
This is the orgin of revolutions, social unrest and social chaos.

Desperation in populations will result in peaceful change or social chaos, bloody civil war or war on neighbors. Let's hope for the peaceful outcome.

3. Demographics: Population and climate changes affect the social order and rulers are seen to be either ineffective or out of touch with the needs of a population and lose adherents.

This can signal massive changes in most of the institutions in the society where powers at the time, including Congress, come to not represent the interests of many of not most of the population. Massive realignments, sudden or gradual in nature, or mass migrations and dislocations can occur, especially if the psychopathic state can no longer provide jobs.

Often, simultaneously, scape-goating occurs where specific races or members of the population are blamed for a disintegrating state of affairs. Or there can be a nice war to divert attention away from the state of affairs.

4. Intercultural contacts and intercultural marriage and mingling: This has always been a change factor, and with the ease of travel, folks can travel and see how other people live and think and make comparisons. Change throughout history has, and always has had this component.

5. Collapse: Upon a close reading of history we see that most times, central authority, simply falls down under its own weight. This is true as regards most of the major civilizations in history. Those

that don't become fragile and the slightest tip has toppled them.

But most often splits in the pyschopathic state where power struggles occur between two powerful factions, occasions the break-up of pyschopathic state.

At some point sustainability becomes impossible.

Meantime see the following on these topics.

Right Now Solutions

http://www.authorsden.com/visit/viewshortstory.asp?id=48285&authorid=121255

Populism Growing

http://www.authorsden.com/visit/viewshortstory.asp?id=59899&authorid=121255

Finances:
http://www.authorsden.com/visit/viewshortstory.asp?id=54668&authorid=121255

Report on Obama

http://www.authorsden.com/visit/viewshortstory.asp?id=48087&authorid=121255

1/15/14 The Democratic Impulse and the
Psychopathic State

In the situation where the psychopathic state falls
down of its own weight, or is defeated in battle,
there are several outcomes observable in history:

The conquered people, or the people formerly
under the yoke of the psychopathic state, usually
embrace the Democratic impulse and want nothing
to do with their erstwhile rulers or psychopathic
structures in society.

Examples:

The Mayan Blood Simple culture fell probably
because of prolonged drought and blood thirsty
ritual murder.

The remaining population did not want to see it
ever come back, irrespective of the skills the

despot society had accrued over time. A simple agrarian society seemed best and that is what we find today across what was formerly the Mayan Empire.

The same is true of the ancient Canaanites, later to be Israelites. Under Egyptian rule for centuries, the Canaanites reinvented themselves and created a strict egalitarian society. They wanted nothing to do with the Pharaoh system seeing it as despotic and they its vassals.

For detail this Israelite history see:

http://www.authorsden.com/visit/viewshortstory.asp?id=47902&authorid=121255

We see similar patterns with the breakup of the Roman Empire, The Mongol Empire, The Russian Empire, and the British Empire-people immediately embrace the Democratic Impulse and want democracy over despotic psychopathic states.

In fact, much of history since biblical times can be seen as the tug back and forth between societies seeking democracy and being conquered by psychopathic rulers which later fall down and to reveal democratic impulses among significant portions of the population.

We see it all over the globe today. It is the freedom-seeking masses vs. those who would seek to dominate their societies and other societies as well. The latter was true even during most of Roman history. It was plebs vs. the Roman Aristocracy.

The corollary of this argument is that however suppressed a given people may be the democratic impulse remains and resurfaces time and time again.

However many individuals in a given society become psychopathic, many, half in modern times, do not succumb to the carrots and sticks offered, or at least tell themselves that their values are not those of their psychopathic leaders.

This clinging to democratic ideals is yet another basis for change and is also why the psychopathic state contains the seeds of its own demise.

How, we want to know in more detail do these trends in fact work themselves out?

1/17/14

If the state can be psychopathic we now look at the existence of a psychopathic state and a psychopathic family or family member looking for connections.

Today we look at the psychopathic and/or Narcissistic family, the mother, or the situation where there is a least one psychopathic personality in the family.

See first:
Family Members

In this first article "bully" in our meaning is the psychopathic member of the family.

"Bullies within the family, especially female bullies, are masters (mistresses?) of manipulation and are fond of manipulating people through their emotions (e.g. guilt) and through their beliefs, attitudes and perceptions. Bullies see any form of vulnerability as an opportunity for manipulation, and are especially prone to exploiting those who are most emotionally needy. Elderly relatives, those with infirmity, illness, those with the greatest vulnerability, or those who are emotionally needy or behaviorally immature family members are likely to be favorite targets for exploitation.

The family bully encourages and manipulates family members etc. to lie, act dishonorably and dishonestly, withhold information, spread misinformation, and to punish the target for alleged infractions, i.e. the family members become the bully's unwitting (and sometimes witting) instruments of harassment.

Bullies are adept at distorting peoples' perceptions with intent to engender a negative view of their target in the minds of family members, neighbors, friends and people in positions of officialdom and authority; this is achieved through undermining, the creation of doubts and suspicions, and the sharing of false concerns, etc. This poisoning of people's minds is difficult to counter, however explaining the game in a calm articulate manner helps people to see through the mask of deceit and to understand how and why they are being used as pawns."

From:
http://www.bullyonline.org/related/family.htm

Now we look at mothers
http://www.youtube.com/watch?feature=player_de tailpage&v=I9Y79a2Ky2s

http://www.youtube.com/watch?feature=player_de tailpage&v=rQmSeyIUvmQ

http://www.youtube.com/watch?feature=player_de tailpage&v=cTLoy_-Yf2E

http://www.youtube.com/watch?feature=player_de

tailpage&v=rJP0FUk6oWY

 http://www.youtube.com/watch?feature=player_d
etailpage&v=lZP6YKnxMHk

 See also the related you tube videos above. They
can give you more detail into this subject.

1/20/14

Varieties of Family Structure

The above can also be analyzed in the context of
how the structure the pyschopathic family looks
and can vary.

See:

http://www.authorsden.com/visit/viewshortstory.as
p?id=49713&authorid=121255www.authorsden.co
m/visit/viewshortstory.asp

 1/22/14
The hot and cold seductive pyschopathic female

https://www.youtube.com/watch?feature=player_d
etailpage&v=y_oAGv_tXHc

-

1/22/14 The Psychopathic Check List

https://www.youtube.com/watch?feature=player_detailpage&v=AIwyvzFaEk4

1/22/14
Psychopaths in Silicon Valley

http://www.businessinsider.com/jerk-tech-founders-often-become-kajillionaires-2014-1

1/31/14

Confessions of a successful female psychopathic attorney.

http://www.psychologytoday.com/articles/201305/confessions-sociopathwww.psychologytoday.com/articles/201305/confessions-sociopath

1/2/14
Ten signs might that you might be in a psychopathic abuse relationship.

http://www.healthcentral.com/schizophrenia/cf/slideshows/10-signs-you-may-be-in-an-emotionally-abusive-relationship?ap=825

1/2/14

http://en.wikipedia.org/wiki/Hare_Psychopathy_Checklist

2/6/14

Can the fearful memories of parents be passed down to the children?

At:

http://www.spring.org.uk/2013/12/fearful-memories-passed-between-generations-through-genetic-code.php#utm_source=feedburner&utm_medium=feed&utm_campaign=Feed%3A+PsychologyBlog+(PsyBlog)

If so this would have enormous implications. More on this in the coming days.

2/6/14

How can you counteract the above and get people to overcome or change their behaviors or their minds.

http://www.spring.org.uk/2012/05/how-to-encourage-people-to-change-their-own-minds.php

2/10/14

Inside the sufferings of the psychopath

http://www.psychiatrictimes.com/psychotic-affective-disorders/hidden-suffering-psychopath-0

It's lonely in there.

http://www.experienceproject.com/stories/Am-Lonely/2703104

2/18/14

Are the mean people on the internet really psychopathic? New study says yes and gives details.

http://www.slate.com/articles/health_and_science/climate_desk/2014/02/internet_troll_personality_study_machiavellianism_narcissism_psychopathy.html

2/25/14

http://www.theguardian.com/science/head-quarters/2014/feb/25/internet-trolls-are-also-real-life-trolls

3/8/14

The Making of a Psychopath--The Invisible Menace

http://www.youtube.com/watch?feature=player_detailpage&v=siuNB5tsZjM

See Also

https://www.youtube.com/watch?feature=player_detailpage&v=nMG1qjpzNPg

How to recognize a psychopath

http://www.youtube.com/watch?v=Gd6P1Ue2aGg&feature=player_detailpage

3/8/14

Psychopaths and Bullies at Work: What to do?

http://www.youtube.com/watch?v=tlB1pFwGhA4&feature=player_detailpage

How to deal with Psychopaths and Bullies and not becoming a thug in return?

http://www.youtube.com/watch?v=sgWyolwBGgE&feature=player_detailpage

Gene Sharp audio Book on how to cope with dictatorships and bullies

http://www.youtube.com/watch?feature=player_detailpage&v=1_UTax4sZ9c

Interview with Gene Sharp.

http://www.youtube.com/watch?feature=player_detailpage&v=ZwuYtzUOcKk

Q and A on psychopaths-video

https://www.youtube.com/watch?feature=player_detailpage&v=_4MEQRgJbfU

Video: More on the female psychopath

https://www.youtube.com/watch?feature=player_detailpage&v=y_oAGv_tXHc

3/22/14

The Bible and Psychopathic Behavior

http://www.history.com/shows/the-bible-rules/videos?mkwid=sFjor2WK1|c_pcrid_42508305438_pkw_the%20bible%20rules_pmt_e&utm_source=google&utm_medium=cpc&utm_term=the%20bible%20rules&utm_campaign=G_The+Bible+Rules&paidlink=1&cmpid=PaidSearch_google_G

The+Bible+Rules_the%20bible%20rules&gclid=C
Mf8wdTPor0CFUWVfgodaWUAEg

See companion piece on Bible

http://www.authorsden.com/visit/viewshortstory.as
p?id=47902&authorid=121255

3/22/14

Fishhead the Movie

http://www.fisheadmovie.com/

Psychopaths in Suits

http://www.forbes.com/sites/victorlipman/2013/04/
25/the-disturbing-link-between-psychopathy-and-
leadership/

http://www.bloombergview.com/articles/2012-01-
03/did-psychopaths-take-over-wall-street-asylum-
commentary-by-william-cohan

Psychopaths in suits-Politicians and Corporate
Types

http://www.springer.com/cda/content/document/cd

a_downloaddocument/fulltext.pdf?SGWID=0-0-45-1269145-p35739432

http://www.theatlantic.com/health/archive/2012/07/the-startling-accuracy-of-referring-to-politicians-as-psychopaths/260517/

The shape of the Narcissistic Mind

http://psychcentral.com/news/2013/07/06/narcissists-lack-of-empathy-tied-to-less-gray-matter/56907.html

Psychopathy and Violence

http://human-nature.com/nibbs/01/psychopathy.html

Brain Scans

http://www.nature.com/news/2007/071212/pdf/450942a.pdf

3/26/14

One of the best psychopath check lists and site I have seen.

https://www.psychopathfree.com/content.php?212-30-Red-Flags

3/28/14

The childhood of psychopaths

http://www.dailymail.co.uk/femail/article-2155489/Is-child-psychopath-Its-common-think--spot-danger-signs-young-three.html

3/29/14

Impulsiveness in Psychopaths

http://www3.psych.purdue.edu/~dlynam/uppspage.htm

3/29/14

 Sex Fantasies of the Narcissist and the Psychopath

 http://www.youtube.com/watch?feature=player_detailpage&v=3LnlT9NlN6I

4/5/14

Sex Lives of Psychopaths

http://www.decision-making-confidence.com/sexual-psychopaths.html

4/5/14

Sex and Psychopath

London School of Economics Video 78 minutes long

http://www.youtube.com/watch?feature=player_de
tailpage&v=8JdGrm3MdHQ

4/5/14

The Ten Types of Disorders

http://www.youtube.com/watch?feature=player_de
tailpage&v=ijMPEgMxras

4/12/14 The Good Side of A Psychopath?

http://www.youtube.com/watch?feature=player_de
tailpage&v=_x8WjkkhSPE

4/27/14

Dating a Psychopath 10 questions to ask.

http://www.huffingtonpost.com/2013/12/07/dating
-a-psychopath_n_4378946.html

5/2/14

Right-Wing-Left-Wing--is this inherited

http://www.alternet.org/why-right-wingers-think-way-they-do-fascinating-psychological-origins-political-ideology?paging=off&current_page=1#bookmark

5/12/14

Psychopaths and Civilizations: New 726 page book on the subject

"In broad scope we witness the history-making leaders in the ancient civilized world, and see the reiteration of psychopathic leadership and personal destinies during the building of contemporary cultures. The individuals, often referred to as Machiavellians, are no less ignoble than the street psychopaths, although they are more intelligent, persuasive, and visionary. From Alexander the Great, and Julius Caesar to Genghis Khan, Napoleon Bonaparte and Mal Tso-Tung, to Joseph Stalin, Adolph Hitler, Fidel Castro, and Che Guevara, we observe the illuminating and often blinding Machiavellian narcissism that works its magic in the creation of innovative governments, as well as in the murder and destructions of generations."

From:

http://darksideofthebrain.com/?page_id=1552

"The short-term mating strategy of the psychopath rejects any and all trait qualities that would tie him to the mating situation, such as empathy, love, guilt, remorse, true confession, cooperation, responsibility, and interest in children. He remains aloof and individualistic on every issue. Non-psychopaths, who strive for long-term mating relations, emphasize traits that the psychopath rejects. That type of male goes for romantic love, commitment, low testosternone behaviors (e.g., child care), low aggression, and non-abusive behaviors that would damage his relations with his partner. He has a communal attitude and sensitivity to all humanitarian processes. Not surprisingly, traits within each strategy are highly correlated: everyone has to be consistent with the others or the harmony is lost, and so are the mating opportunities with the female. For instance, psychopaths tend to be promiscuous, glib, charming, competitive, risk-taker, self-confident, and narcissistic, all in contrast to those traits of non-psychopaths."

From:

http://darksideofthebrain.com/?p=403

5/14/14

The Cool Girl, Iconic Career Psychopath-Sociopath

http://digg.com/2014/the-female-sociopath

5/22/14

Can a child be a psychopath

http://www.nytimes.com/2012/05/13/magazine/can-you-call-a-9-year-old-a-psychopath.html?pagewanted=all&_r=0

The 12 signs of a child psychopath? True or not?

http://www.hlntv.com/article/2013/08/23/teens-who-kill

More on adult psychopaths--Australians

http://www.youtube.com/watch?feature=player_detailpage&v=JWqZQw0itTg

http://www.youtube.com/watch?feature=player_detailpage&v=srXqIh_0qpg

Psychopaths in History

http://www.authorsden.com/visit/viewshortstory.asp?id=60893&authorid=121255

Character Disturbance

http://www.youtube.com/watch?feature=player_detailpage&v=grXxRRbtZ2A

5/23/14

The Manipulative Personality

https://www.youtube.com/watch?feature=player_detailpage&v=srXqIh_0qpg

More:

https://www.youtube.com/watch?feature=player_detailpage&v=94Uie7UCdOU

5/23/14

Psychopathic Elements in Human Society-At the Top

http://www.youtube.com/watch?feature=player_detailpage&v=_I87hC8dcVU

6/2/14

http://www.kpfa.org/archive/id/103339

Volume two of Psychopaths in One Month and daily subscription updates available. See www.lonniehicks.com for details.

www.ingramcontent.com/pod-product-compliance
Lightning Source LLC
Chambersburg PA
CBHW060222290526
45789CB00003B/1378